From Hell and Back: A Journey of Loss and Love

Charles M. Brown

Published by Charles Brown, 2024.

While every precaution has been taken in the preparation of this book, the publisher assumes no responsibility for errors or omissions, or for damages resulting from the use of the information contained herein.

FROM HELL AND BACK: A JOURNEY OF LOSS AND LOVE

First edition. May 28, 2024.

ISBN: 979-8224695911

Written by Charles M. Brown.

Table of Contents

Love is a blessing and a curse. With the right person you can move the earth, with the wrong one you can lose yourself completely. Find the one that would burn all of eternity to see you safe and successful. Then .. let them burn the world to ashes to see it fit your desires. Find your Tsune.

Scarlett, you have taken me to places I could have never dreamed of, and encouraged me to become the best father and partner I could be. Thank you for showing me that I can accomplish my dreams.

Act One: The End Of Love

Sometimes we fall for the idea of a person, not the actual person themselves. When that happens we can start to overlook things that we would normally never accept. These things can sometimes turn into abuse. So when they want to go.... Let them. It's hard but if you can, choose yourself. Be your own hero. Save yourself.

Paths

I lost my love the other day.
Had she died, I could accept.
Had sickness rended us, this I could heal.
Had sadness separated us, this I could take.
But she went right on her path,
And I went left on mine.
I did not know our paths had split,
Till I saw her lips on another.
She did not speak,
Just turned and smiled as I broke in grief.
I lost my love the other day.
For she went right on her path,
And I went left on mine.

Broken On My Floor

Lying broken on the floor,
My heart shattered by my grief.
It felt like only yesterday,
That I said goodbye,
And watched you walk away.
Lying broken on my floor,
I wept and screamed in my pain.
A flood of rending sadness,
That felt as though it would never pass.
Lying broken on the floor,
I prayed that this sadness passed.
Days, then weeks did pass,
But slowly my pain did ease.
And I stood from that floor one day this October past.
With each step toward door my door,
Alas did I grow stronger.
And as the shadows grew longer upon the floor,
I could hear my weeping past, and finally, no more.
As I move forward into the light
May the shadows comfort the shade I left weeping,
Broken on my floor.

Beneath These Stars.

How many nights have I sat,
Beneath these very stars,
And thought of nothing,
But of the last time I saw you?
So angry, so proud, so defiant.
So full of hate for me,
Who you once loved.
Beneath these very stars I waited,
As you shared yourself with others.

You Did Not Hear

I said goodbye yet you did not hear,
I said I love you yet you did not feel.
I begged you to change yet you stayed the same.
I grew to become the one you needed,
You devolved into toxicity.
I strived to make you smile,
And felt tears burn my eyes.
I gave you my soul,
And you left me barren and alone.
I craved the heat of your touch,
And you denied me the light of your flame.
I said goodbye long after you left,
Yet you did not hear.

I Did Not See

I loved you as though we were pure,
I did not see our corruption.
I needed you to be my light in the dark,
I did not see you were the cause of my night.
I hungered for your touch,
I did not see your desire for any but me.
I worked to heal you,
I did not see that you were destroying me.
As an addict chases their needle,
You were the sweet destruction I did not need.
I wanted you forever,
I did not see that I was but a moment in your eternity.

Flames

I should have known though I did not see,
You spoke though in soliloquy.
My passion poured through my breast,
Only to break upon your sophistry.
Though I gave sweet words,
Returned to me was only hate.
Your eyes burned with the fire of passion,
But it was only your zeal for my conflagration.
Though I grew weak in what I felt was love,
You grew strong by my eradication.

Act Two: Battle Of Will

Everyone tells you to save yourself, but no one tells you about the process after. Not that it's lonely, or that it hurts. Not that looking in the mirror is hard because honestly you can't stand yourself for allowing yourself to be treated the way that you were, only to see them going off to be happy like you never existed, even if they aren't.

In Peace

We grow not in peace but in pain.
We stand stagnant in our happiness.
We live complacent in our loves.
We sit still in our positivity.
But....
We move forward in our grief,
We burn brighter in our hate.
We grow faster as our tears fall.
We evolve in our pain, not our peace.

I Dreamed of Love

Beneath the stars I dreamed of love,
And from the dark she came.
Between the trees she glided,
And gently stepped to me.
Beneath the heavy bows I lay transfixed,
As true love moved to me.
With only the twinkling eternity above as witness,
Fair did she grant me a kiss.
With passion did I start from sleep,
To find myself alone.
And wept did I for the folly of finding love,
In that quiet forest of dreams.
So now, an old man, do I lay beneath the stars,
To dream of my love true and fair,
Before I surrender to the night.

Why

Why wasn't I enough for you to stay?
To find yourself in my love?
Why did you feel the need to leave?
To lose yourself in the night?
Why did you walk away?
To fade from my sight?
Why weren't we enough to keep you?
To leave us in despair and pain?
Why did you deny my heart?
To find your broken way?

Alone

We wander in a wilderness,
Bereft and alone in a forest of pain.
I scream your name and silent echoes return.
Alone in the mists of time and pain,
Trapped in my mind, longing for you.
My heart lies shattered upon the earthen floor,
Your silence echoes in infinity.
For I took one path and you another,
And though we both wander in a wilderness,
We wander, separate and alone.

Parting

Our parting was not by chance,
But fated and forced by your malice.
Capricious though your heart,
Cancerous was your desire.
And though I was not innocent,
Nor was I prepared for your lie.
Would I have known your blight,
Could I have guarded my heart?
Fated and forced was our parting,
Not by chance but by your arrogance.
Come to me, whether in darkness or in light.

Slaves of love

The jagged soul from silken lies,
Cries yield to sophistry.
A hunger steals for miles,
For a love quenched only in desire.
The silence in need wars within a torn breast.
A heart sundered by the pain,
The corruption of lust.
Lost in the winds of a cosmos unchanged,
By the screams of the damned.
Those slaves of love.

Oceans

An ocean of emotions pour over me, through me.
Heavy is my sadness,
Washed upon the tides of my soul.
Pulled to sea, rended and torn a battered mind,
Screams of anguish muffled by the breaking sea.
Deep thrumming fills my senses,
Of love lost and never reborn.
Salt fills my lungs and quenches my raging heart,
Its fires slowly extinguished,
and slowly the tide returns me.
The churning sea soothes my shattered psyche,
Heals my pyretic wounds, and gives me....back to me.

Find Me Not

Love seeks me like a mad huntress.
Lost in a forest of feelings,
Branches of memory whip my face,
In my limitless flight.
Running, fearing, weeping
Starving for love yet terrified of its visage.
Stumbling alone through the night,
Fleeing my own memories.
Love seeks me, hunts me, Yet I flee in fright.
For though I crave love,
I fear more, its pain.
Love seeks me in the forest of night,
Yet finds me not for my fear, my pain,
Resides in my breast.
Love, though I yearn for your embrace,
May you find me not.

Act Three: Healing

Once you start healing, you go through all these stages. It's almost like you're grieving in a way, not that you're grieving your ex, but grieving the parts of you that got lost along the way. The missed opportunities, the adventures, the life experiences, and sadly the things you used to love. You become weary about new relationships, and future partners. They must be after something, are you just lonely, what if they hurt you again? Healing is just as difficult as letting go, but sometimes a person just falls in love with all the broken pieces of you, and becomes determined to be your superglue.

Love Found Me

Love Found me black and broken.
Unable to see, to hear,
To feel past my madness.
In my despair she reached for me.
In my loneliness she comforted me.
In my brokenness she held my pieces,
As they fell to the floor.
She held me there until I stopped shaking.
And then with gentle hands she put the pieces back.
With gentle words she soothed my grief,
With songs sung softly she eased my soul.
When I was ready, still barely healed,
And mildly stable, she showed me that,
Though I was not the man I had been,
I was a new man standing with her.
And when I could, I offered her my pieces,
All that I had left to love.
She loved the pieces that were left,
And grew new ones to replace the old.
Love found me black and broken.
But nursed me till I was whole.

Where Do We Go From Here

Where do we go from here?
A nameless void of possibility.
From sunset to sunrise possibility and probability,
Burning through us like starlight.
Vast oceans of time and space,
And choice being our only guide.
Winds of change blowing through our lives,
In what direction shall we seek?
Where do we go from here,
With none to plot our course,
But our own whim or desire?
Betwixt nor between where do we go from here?
Let us plot our own course.

Show me

Show me what love is.
I beg for your caress.
I cry for your attention.
I pray for your thoughts.
I seek for your heart.
I lust for your mind.
I weep for your gaze.
Show me what love is,
For I am alone without you.

Two worlds

To love the darkness and the light.
To hunger for your caress.
To lust for your mind.
To resonate from the sound of your voice.
Two worlds in human form,
trapped in each other's gravity.
Spinning brightly in the darkness.
Burning everywhere we touch.
Simultaneously exploding and melding together.
Pushing away and drawing towards.
Two worlds becoming one,
In the emptiness of our fate.

Cage

A gift in a gilded cage,
Did you come to me?
Broken from your wars,
Your soul streaked with the soot of pain.
The decay of being unseen,
unwanted, and betrayed.
I saw you there upon the floor,
I reached for you to give you peace,
I opened your cage to free you from your past,
I loved you as I protected you.
A gift, but free in grace.
In love shines your beauty, free for all time.

Agony of Pleasure

A touch that burns,
The yearning of passion.
A thousand nerves bright with pain.
An agony of pleasure.
A heat encapsulated by need.
A billion stars forming,
Scorching in their need for release.
A wrath of desire seeking its peace.
A hunger for oneness to consume the soul.

New Dawn

We all walk in the dark.
Of wars fought and loves lost.
We scream and we mourn,
In the tempest of our growth.
And in the darkest part of night,
A new light is born.
From our woe and anguish,
New beginnings are formed.
One star dies so another may rise.
In the silence of night,
A new dawn is born.

Loves Home

Lust was my shield,
But love, did I find.
We came together in passion,
Yet I was cast away.
We hungered for each other's touch,
Yet I was left starving and alone.
But through the tears and pain,
Did love find me again?
It came to me as though a dream,
And held me in my anguish.
Love cherished me when I had no worth.
Love destroyed my soul,
And later, made its home in me.

I Remain

You left me lost and alone.
My thoughts, my dreams, torn asunder.
My heart, bleeding and broken in my chest.
Yet I remain.
I faced the madness of my despair.
I wore my tears upon my face,
I screamed my pain.... alone.
Yet I remain.
I stood stupidly in the rain.
I watched you love another.
I held myself silent and still in the dark.
Yet I remain.
And slowly I stood once again.
And slowly I smiled once again.
And slowly I loved once again.
For, to this day,
I remain!

Bluesman

The plucking of the old guitar stirs my soul,
As the gaze of my lover warms my lust.
The gentle twang from the steel strings,
Teases my ear as her fingers kiss my skin.
The notes of the old steel guitar soothe my mind,
As her breath on my neck warms my soul.
The croaking of the blues man's voice,
A descant to her warm contralto.
The blues man's dark notes rest in my breast,
As her love lays its claws into me.
Here I stand, crossroads bound,
With a woman on my arm and a bluesman
Playing rusty notes down the road.

Act Four: Love Lives Again

When the whole process starts you sort of swear off relationships for a bit. Tons of reasons, loads of reasons to never invest in another person because... people suck, no really read this and tell me that there isn't a single person you met in your life, that didn't just suck at existing. Then there are people, like HER. The best part is, you knew who I was talking about and I didn't have to say it, even if it's a guy you knew. They just make the world a better place, show you a different side to the world, and suddenly you see that the world didn't suck, just your view of it. She makes it better.

Maiden Fair

My maiden, fair, is a warrior.
At my side does she walk,
My equal and my shield.
For no greater love hath I,
Than to fight beside her as the sun rides high,
And love her fiercely in our furs beneath the moon.
Many ladies may wear jewels,
but she is bedecked in the scars of her honor.
For no greater gift can a warrior give,
than the burning of the love inside her.
My maiden fair is a warrior,
And she is the master of my heart.

Little Fox

My Fox of many tails guides me in the forest.
Her soft glowing fur a beacon,
Among the gloomy ferns.
Her gentle foot falls,
Like whispers on the earth.
Lost would I be among the brambles and thorns,
Were she not there to care for me.
Starving and alone she found me,
And with a glint in her eye she gathered me.
Towards home she guides me, this little fox,
So that never again will I be alone.

Hiraeth-(For Tsune)
I see my home in your eyes,
The sound of your voice is sweet to my soul.
The brush of your fingertip ,
ignites a lust I've never known.
Your Soul sets my senses alight.
Your embrace is my safe place.
A touch, a word, a lover's caress,
Is a boon greater than gold.
When I was lost you were my light.
When I hurt you were my balm.
When my heart was shattered,
You were the one who held me in the night.
In a thousand days of torment,
You were my only surcease.
I see my home in your eyes,
For with you I find grace.

Lust Turned Love

A lust turned love.
Held together with chains of desire and pain.
Souls melding and healing ,
in the fire of our need.
Once torn and wrent now made whole.
In a love born from the ashes of misery.
Two lost souls who hungered,
Now joined in union as night to day.
With tears we spent our screams of pain,
With gasps and moans ,
we painted the stars with our need.
A lust turned love that healed our days,
And made a universe all our own.

Burn

We burn brightly in the night,
Of darkest dreams made real.
To climb the heights of pleasure,
From the twilight of our souls.
We light the night with our fire,
burning away all between us.
Two souls melding and molten,
In the furnace of our love.
Two become one in our forging desire,
Souls lost in the shadows,
Who now burn brightly with the night.

Wicked

I am made wicked by your presence.
I am made wicked by the light in your eyes.
I am made wicked by the smell of your hair.
I am made wicked by the grace of your smile.
I am made wicked by the sweetness of your laugh.
I am made wicked by the kindness of your soul.
I am made wicked by my love for you.
And I am undone.

Dance

We dance in the moonlight,
Basking beneath its silver brilliance.
Sensuous movements joined by touch.
The touch of bodies and of souls.
Thralls to the music but slaves to our love,
We move in the night.
A twist, a dip, yet our dance remains,
Lovers lost to the refrain.
The smell of jasmine, the sound of thunder.
Atop our mountain we move with the rhythm.
Our sight, our touch, our dance,
Creates heat shimmering in the air and in being.
Two lovers, two loves, joined in the night.

Hungry Thoughts

Your words stir hungry thoughts.
Your voice whispers erotic poetry to my soul.
Your lips drip lust like divinity.
Your speech and your pause drive my pulse.
Dark thoughts and lustful deeds,
Create our sexual symmetry.
Intimacy creates telepathy,
And I yearn for the experience.
You make me wicked,
Delirious in my desire.

Craving

My craving for your touch leaves me writhing.
Locked in longing but by the sound of your voice.
Erotic thoughts caress my cortex,
As my wantonness spreads.
A taste of wild cherries on my tongue,
The taste of your carnality.
A dark need throbs just within my veins,
To hear those soft noises only meant for me.
Libidinous I rise,
My need a lewdness to stain your skin.
My need throbs sensual in my bones,
Aching for your warm embrace.

Act 5: Falling deeper

After everything you go through in leaving bad relationships, it's hard to want to trust again. To really fall for the person because you feel like there is no safety net. What if it happens again?What if it's worse? The 'what ifs' will eat you alive. Sometimes you just have to fall and enjoy the ride.

Two Touches

Blues music strains through the speakers,
Caressing my mind as you do my skin.
Loving touches in both directions,
Soothing my soul and easing my aches.
Gentle notes touch my temples,
As your breath warms my skin.
Soft desire plays through me,
As the touch of my two loves
Guide my soul to peace.

Altar

I worship at your altar,
Dark rainy nights and candlelight.
Your scent sits on my tongue,
Sweet in the relief only you may grant.
A supplicant I stand before you,
To worship in caress and kiss.
We linger in our lust,
Each a temple of need.
Desire burns in our skin,
And ignites our touch.
Let us worship together,
In the holiness of our decadence.

Sonic Baptism

Sonic baptism blesses my nerves.
Sacred notes bathe me in redemption,
Save me from my pain,
Save me from myself.
The music grants grace to my weary soul,
A thousand notes give peace to a million tears.
A temple of sound to free me.

Safe

The wind howls madly in the night.
It's screams fuel dreams,
Of scare and fright.
But sheltered are we,
From such madness,
Entwined in touch and caress.
No storm may rage,
No Demon shall challenge,
As we hold to our storm,
Our tempest of love.
And though the trees shake,
And the boughs do creak,
We feel no fear,
As the darkness grows near.
For the wind will howl,
And screams may echo,
But we are safe forever.

Stygian Night

Towers of pain and centuries of despair,
Spark aching visions without repair.
The Stygian night echoes in screams,
A million souls begging for surcease.
A simple anesthesia to ease lifes agony,
Is a dream sought but never found.
We cry in darkness side by side,
But separated by a chasm of the mind.
NIghtmares abound in our personal hells,
But there is no release.
A simple touch to unite the damned,
A reverie of the lost wishing to be found.

Ecstasy of Sound

Sonic orgasms shriek through me.
Pounding notes embed in my marrow.
Sinuous sound coils along my muscles.
Delicious lyrics pluck at my sinews.
Do I play the music,
Or does it play me?
A demon rests behind my eyes,
As fingers bleed and hands do cramp.
Lost in the lust of synergy,
The melody writhes unbidden.
Transfixed in my compulsion,
Impaled upon my desire,
An ecstasy of sound arouses me.

Hellhounds

Hellhounds chase me in my dreams.
Their howls haunt my waking hours.
I smell their feted breath on my neck.
Night or day I feel their teeth,
Snapping at my heels.
Not the darkness,
Nor the brightest day,
Hides my track.
No nation sack protects me,
No gris gris to guard me.
I run through the night,
Run to the crossroads.
Across the tracks and through the river,
But I cannot escape them.
Red eyes and razor teeth,
I fear how they shall rend me.
What dark deal has set them to me?
What hoodoo man can save me?

Act 6: The one

After everything is said and time has done its job, you come to realize you may have found the one. Your person who will pick you up and drive you to be the best you that you can be. Once you find this person, love them and grow alongside them. See where your dreams take you.

Staccato

Erotic beats thrill the night,
As we two dance to rhythmic drums.
Our bodies move to the staccato demand,
Our first foreplay upon this stage.
We mirror our movements upon the floor,
As prelude for later proclivities.
Our chests heave and pulses race;
As, gasping, we will be naked under the stars.
Foreshadowing our true cravings.
Our appetite for the dance,
Is but a poor contemplation of our fantasies.

Midnight Spires

Midnight spires hover in the moonlight.
Nightmarish in their architecture.
Ghouls and gargoyles peer beneath the eaves,
Staring at me from in my dreams.
And whence stands the spires of this tower?
In my mind, in my dreams.
But should I ever go there,
And see the gleam from lofty heights,
Surely will I lose myself in its decadence.
Of fantasy are these gothic lances,
Piercing the frail night sky.
But one day, this place too shall I see.

High

High moments and halcyon dreams.
My only drug is your love for me.
Your touch speeds my pulse,
You show me that I am alive.
Once broken but now healed,
A junkie from a relationship's toxicity.
Now I am home,
Held truly and safe,
In true love's embrace.

Moon Flow

She dances in the dark,
As moonlight kisses her skin.
The very air a caress.
Free in her love of the night,
Her passion flows in movement.
Sinuous curves undulate
With a dark passion,
Her rhythm an embrace.
Longingly the stars look down upon her,
Lust written in the sky.
She dances in the dark,
To music all her own.

In Shadow

On a ridge silhouetted by the moon,
Stands a Lady in a black cloak.
Though I cannot see her face,
Her attributes frighten me.
She stands tall, ominous, dangerous,
In that silver light.
She does not speak but I know her call.
I know not whether she be a Maiden,
Or whether she is a Mother, or the Crone.
But I stand in fear of her all the same.
A ravens caw, the moonlights kiss,
She stands tall in her shadow.

Ignite My Mind

Ignite my mind with your words.
Burn my soul with your passion.
Tell me slowly what you desire.
Make me long for your voice.
Let me hunger for your thoughts.
Grant me your fantasies.
Dance among my imaginings.
Scorch me with your lust.
Rage within my mind.

Riffs

Guitar riffs scorch my mind,
A demonic musician strums madly,
Willing my mind to writhe.
Tortured notes invade my spirit,
Guiding me places I've never been.
It's mad song compels me,
Drives me to release my pain.
A tempo scorching my marrow,
Absolves me of fear.
Every pause, every pluck of heated strings,
Sends me further into frenzy,
Further into peace.
It's dark symphony frees me,
Pushing me to become one with the music.

The Hill

The Dark Lady stands on her crest,
Atop a hill lit by an ancient moon.
Her beauty has never been seen,
Yet all feel her presence.
She stands witness, this Dark Lady,
To woe and love, passion and sorrow;
But apart from the mortal frame.
Oh, frailty of years she does not know,
Immortal she stands under her willow tree.
Framed in shadow she watches,
Shrouded in a land where few remain.
Her legend lost, her story hidden,
None remember from whence she came.
But this, the Dark Lady knows as truth.
She will stand atop her hill and listen,
Listen to life's sweet refrain.

Masochism

Masochism is freedom in despair,
Dejected souls find meaning in the pain.
For if we are trapped in our emptiness,
Is it not fair to exchange one pain for another?
Life is but endless misery,
So should we not find release,
By choosing our favorite torment?
And could anguish felt so keenly,
Not be given such beautiful form?
To give grace and beauty,
In such despondency?

Human Enigma

Love is the province of the damned.
Not the dead, for that would be safer.
Love is a drug filling the veins,
With pyrotechnic delusions.
For at the end one's body burns,
One's soul is blackened by it's blaze,
With no hope of quenching.
More souls have been condemned,
More cries for mercy given to escape love,
Than all the dead in Hell begging for release.
Like any drug love is oh so addictive,
And rots one from core to skin.
Save me from love lost,
But grant me love once again.
The human enigma made manifest.

Passion

Passion turns nova in endless twilight,
A beacon in the fog and gloom.
So raw and elemental,
defying the umbra of despair.
In a reality of despondency,
Purity creates life from pain.
An art to this in defying the roles,
Cast upon us by hateful fate.
So burn brightly like the sun,
To chase away the darkness of Sheol.

Red Sheets

Dark red satin sheets grace my bed,
As visions of you writhe in my head.
Sensual memories entwine of our trysts,
As carnally as our bodies lying here.
The glide of my skin along these sheets,
Is an arousing reminder of your skin on mine.
My soft lewd moans of pleasure,
Creates mental echoes of our past.
The fabric is as soft to my fingers,
As your delicious body was under mine.
Oh, how I long to have you,
On such red satin sheets.

Filigree

I sit in a bed with purple sheets.
The walls are black with silver filigree.
And in this bed have I spent countless hours,
Worshiping every part of you.
The taste of your skin,
The smell of your hair,
Fuel my forbidden fantasies.
In our wanton debauchery we created realities.
Worlds of pleasure and worlds of pain,
Worlds of intimacy between just us two.
I long for you once again,
Mounted high upon this bed,
To receive your sensual sacrament.
Growls and moans echo from the walls,
From our willing debasement.
Wonton are we united in lust,
To feel each other's end.

Act 7: Healing

At this stage you think you have everything under control, but sometimes the past will come back to remind you where you have been. You have everything going for you, and then wham, your very own instant reminder. But in these moments it's ok to remember that we all need time to heal and that everyone moves at their own pace.

Though She Be Gentle

Though she be gentle in her night,
She is fierce in her desire.
Molten lust burns brightly,
Along skin yearning for her lover.
Her thirst for carnality,
Rides the air like devine perfume.
Appetite sings through her veins,
Scorching with so dark a need.
Lascivious thoughts fuel her mind,
Rough fantasies buried in her soul.
Her body aches for union,
Consummation of her mind's compulsion.
Though she be gentle in her night,
Craving drives her cupidity.

Oracles

Oracles described our love,
Birthed in passion and pain.
A hundred lives and a thousand tears,
I survived to find you.
Countless roads I walked,
For just the scent of you.
Lifetimes I stood waiting,
Just to pass you in the night.
Death I suffered countless times,
To be reborn trying to find you.

Thorns

A romance born of thorns.
The gentle pricks drew our blood,
And grew our love.
Tears shed stained the petals,
And gave glory in its beauty.
A rose grown strong in passion,
Seeded in pain.

Solace

We danced under the stars in love and pain.
Vines crossing from the forest to our souls.
We danced hungry for the other's touch.
We raged at the emptiness in our souls.
We hungered for the fire in our eyes.
We wept in the emptiness of our pain.
We gloried in the warmth of our love.
We two, banished, found solace in the other.
We two wept to feed the forest,
And in turn the forest fed our souls.
We danced under the stars,
In love and pain,
And found solace in our love together.

Surcease

I lie between her legs nuzzled in her embrace.
She strokes my hair with a gentle touch,
Her caress permits my soul to rest.
Softness comes with each new breath,
As I bask cradled near her safest place.
Worries and woes drain from my soul,
Pressed within the heat of her thighs.
I find solace from my weary mind,
Our limbs mingled and entwined
I long for these moments of soft embrace,
So that I might find surcease.

Sunny Day

I saw you once as you walked away,
And never had I seen such beauty.
Though I thought you walked it was a sway,
As you headed on your way.
For years I longed for a sight of you,
But you did not return after that day.
Now am I old and gray with years,
Yet still I hold the vision,
Of love lost on a sunny day.

Nature's Gold

To hold your hand among the sacred Elm,
And cherish our kisses along the trail.
I watch you stop and examine the plants,
Knowing nature's greatest beauty stands with me.
We share our love among the leaves,
And watch the flowers bloom with its seed.
Our passions stoke in the umbra of the Oak,
We two love ferociously.
And as we wander through the paths,
We feed our souls with nature's greatest gold.

Reflections

Reflections and echoes are all that remain,
Of a love once pure but now tainted.
I can see what was in the mirror of my mind.
I can hear our laughter in the stillness.
Yet all that remains is darkness and dust.
And so I must move forward.
Away from the dark and bravely,
Into the light of a new future.
I must yet let my grieving be done,
So that I can live once more.
I must smash the mirrors.
I must scream to drown the echoes.
I shall fight my way to living.
For no good comes dwelling amongst ghosts.
Life moves forward and so shall I.

Loves me

She grants me peace in my storm.
Beaten by the tempest of life,
Burdened and weary I walk,
She grants me absolution.
Yet she grants me reason.
Defeated I stand in my arena,
My soul lost to nihilism,
Again she heals me of my wounds.
I find faith at her altar.
As agonies make me frail,
She rebuilds my soul with kindness.
A greater creature I shall never know,
Than she who loves me and myself alone.

Longing

In the darkest hours of night,
I hunger for your touch.
At the loneliest hours,
My skin aches for your caress.
On the coldest sheets,
I still feel your warmth.
Along my red satin pillow,
I can still smell your skin.
Once again I hunger for the taste of you,
As one starving in the moonlight.
Without you beside me,
I long for your return.

Soft Rain

Soft rain falls to the earth,
Like tears from an absent lover.
Gentle aches trace the skin,
Like rivers from a downpour.
Longing blows through me,
As the sighing of the trees.
The sudden pang of the heart,
A lightning bolt from the sky.
Echoes of sadness past,
Is the distant thunder from the clouds.
A storm passed but still fresh,
Pain that fades but brings new life.

To Write

The words whisper to me.
From my mind and from the page.
They call to me to be written.
Images dance within my consciousness,
Aching to burst forth into the world.
My passion, my obsession,
Such dark bliss to write.
These words show worlds,
Realities beyond comprehension.
To write is the darkest pleasure,
And the greatest bliss.

My Muse

My muse calls to me.
Where fairies dance and brooks do sing.
Where trees walk and mountains dance.
Under skies not yet described.
Where oceans hold cities,
And where deserts dance with rain.
She calls me to impossible places,
And never before seen dreams.
In worlds no other has seen,
She expresses a philosophy of life.
My muse calls to me,
To give life to worlds unglimpsed.

Act 8: Moving on

The time comes when you realize that traumatic breakups never really leave you. They just get easier to deal with. Time heals you and helps you grow, you realize that the person who accepted those behaviors is gone and you are a new version of yourself. This version of you moves and breathes, lives and grows ever moving forward.

Sandy Shores

We touch and kiss on sandy shores.
The mist adorns our laughing lips.
A gentle sun to guide our steps,
We trail the sand, hand in hand.
To watch the surf beat the breakers,
And sit embraced to watch such beauty.
And though the sun will set upon this coast,
Never shall our love see such dimming.

Though She Be Gone

Though she be gone for many years,
Memories of our love do sustain me.
Though she be gone long days hence,
Ever will her name be etched upon my soul.
Though she be gone her whispered words remain,
Such words do still keep me sane.
Though she be gone I feel her touch,
And miss not her final words of love.
Though she be gone and her shade long passed,
Her love keeps me bound upon this mortal plane.

Walk Through The Woods

To walk through the woods,
And sit beneath an old pine tree.
To watch the sun shine through the branches.
And the small shadows among the roots,
Who knows what treasures are hidden there.
To feel the breeze blow through the trees,
And hear the boughs shake and rattle.
To walk in the shade and in the light,
And feel such life connects with me.
To walk through the woods is a balm to the soul,
For no matter what age you think you've seen,
They are all far older than thee or me.

Ancient Tree

Sitting at the roots of an ancient tree,
I did hear a whisper come to me.
It came faintly on the breeze,
And softly sang to me.
I looked around among the roots,
But could not see its source.
And though it's voice was faint,
It's trill was clear within my ear.
I stumbled and fell wrapped around the thorns,
To find a shadow which whispered a song,
That held me deep within its thrawl.
And at the foot of that ancient tree,
Wasted did I to root and maw.
Long do my bones lay on the forest floor,
But still I can hear that ancient song.

A Cabin

A cabin in our forest,
Nestled near brook and tree.
The gentle rush of water,
The swaying of the trees.
Find us two there,
Cradled in the shadow.
Hidden among wood and dirt,
More ancient than we.
And as the breeze flows,
To weave and blow,
The leaves of yesteryear.
My longing for our cabin,
Deep within the forest,
Fills me with need.
For our peace is found,
Among the eldest trees.

Perfect World

A cabin in the woods.
The light of a campfire in your eyes.
Dancing under the trees to an old radio.
Holding hands and gentle conversation.
The winds grow and drive us in.
Cuddled beneath fur blankets,
As need grows between us.
Moonlight glistens off your skin,
As you writhe under me.
Intimacy as complete as our union,
We drift asleep in a perfect world.

Don't miss out!

Visit the website below and you can sign up to receive emails whenever Charles M. Brown publishes a new book. There's no charge and no obligation.

https://books2read.com/r/B-A-HOQMC-AFHID

BOOKS 2 READ

Connecting independent readers to independent writers.

Did you love *From Hell and Back: A Journey of Loss and Love*?
Then you should read *Gaeth's Redemption*[1] by Charles M.
Brown!

[2]

**"You always warned me that being queen would mean my
death." - Simone**

A romantic war story that starts when Gaeth a man with a
war-torn heart, meets Simone a woman too afraid to become
queen. With losses accrued on both sides, the couple struggles to
find a balance between the magical chemistry within them and
the catastrophic destiny that awaits them. Gathe's Redemption
features yokai, witches, descriptive battles, and some spicey

---

1. https://books2read.com/u/4EB7Gg

2. https://books2read.com/u/4EB7Gg

scenes all coming together to show that the lines of war and lust are not all that different.

Read more at https://www.hellhoundsrun.com/.

About the Author

Charles Brown is the creator of Hellhound's Run, a universe where the imposible becomes possible, and the adventures are endless. The Hellhound Verse follows adventures through creepy pastas and novels alike exploring all walks of life within the univers and meeting the entities within.

Charlie also enjoys writing poetry that explores deep human emotions within everyday occurences. From leaving abusive relationships to finding real love, enjoying the simplicity of a front porch and good blues.

He spent over twenty five years in public service as a Law Enforcement Officer and 911 Telecommunicator before rediscovering his dream of writing. He has previously won several awards for his poetry in his youth and is greatly enjoying bringing his new works to life.

Read more at https://linktr.ee/Hellhoundsrun.